Every Day May Not Be Good...
But There is Something
Good in Every Day

A Collection of Poems

– JOCELYN SHAFFER –

An environmentally friendly book printed and bound in England by
www.printondemand-worldwide.com

Mixed Sources
Product group from well-managed
forests, and other controlled sources
www.fsc.org Cert no. TT-COC-002641
© 1996 Forest Stewardship Council

PEFC Certified
This product is
from sustainably
managed forests
and controlled
sources
www.pefc.org
PEFC/16-33-415

www.fast-print.net/store.php

Every Day May Not Be Good... But There is
Something Good in Every Day: A Collection of Poems
Copyright © Jocelyn Shaffer 2013

A catalogue record for this book is available from the British Library

ISBN 978-178035-598-6

First published 2013 by
FASTPRINT PUBLISHING
Peterborough, England.

Every Day May Not Be Good...

I want to make a difference

I want to make a difference
A memory to live on
Something I can leave behind
A memory when I'm gone

I want to make a difference
It should be something good
It should be quite remarkable
Just like a good deed should

I want to make a difference
Something folks will say
She was quite amazing
The best in every way

I want to make a difference
Whatever shall it be
Achieving a diploma
Or gaining a degree

I want to make a difference
I wonder what to do
Coming top in all I can
And helping others too

I want to make a difference
When the time is right
Helping others every day
To make their future bright

I want to make a difference
I wonder if I can
Daughter, sister, wife and Mum
And recently a Gran

I want to make a difference
Always try my best
I'll do all I can for you
Just put me to the test

I want to make a difference
Please tell me what to do
If you need a helping hand
Then I'll be there for you

I want to make a difference
Before it is too late
To do something amazing
Something really great

I want to make a difference
But the truth is plain to see
I don't need to change a thing
Just keep on being me!

Noise

Something that we all endure
An onslaught to our ears
Incessant music when we're out
It brings us close to tears

We cannot get away from it
In shopping malls and bars
Nor in the street, as we can hear
Noise blaring out from cars

The boutiques are the very worst
The music there is deafening
There is no hiding place for us
It shows no sign of lessening

Loud music all around us
The volume turned up high
It pounds away and drives you mad
It makes you want to cry

But even then, when you get home
The noise will not abate
Dogs are barking, babies crying,
And teenagers out late

And just when you get some peace
And everything is calm
You're sleeping, but are woken up
By a neighbour's burglar alarm

3

There are things that should be loud
Like Ambulance, Fire and Police
And how could we all survive
If their sirens ever cease

And when we go to watch a match
It just wouldn't be the same
If when a player scores a goal
There's no cheering at the game

And when we see a pop star
Especially if we're fans
We show how much we like them
When we clap our hands

So, noise we'll have to tolerate
For many, many years
Unless we buy a large supply
Of ear plugs, for our ears!

Time

One priceless thing in this life
That we just can't deny
Is something that we all need
That money just can't buy

It can't be held, it can't be stopped
Nor stolen, lost or found
It isn't large, it isn't small
It does not make a sound

You may be wondering what it is
That we can't grasp or see
It is time, that can't stand still
I'm sure you will agree

We just can't hurry time on
Is something we all know
When you want the time to fly
The minutes go so slow

Time is of the essence
And we should never wait
'Cos if we don't do it now
It will be too late

They say time waits for no man
And this is very true
So make sure you have the time
For things you need to do

Every Day May Not Be Good...

There's no time like the present
And we should make it count
And use it very wisely
So that we're not timed out

At night, time passes slowly
Right up until sun rise
Some people say that time stands still
And others say time flies

Some people say they don't have time
Yet others have too much
So please make sure you make the time
To always keep in touch

Please make time for others
We really have to try
As if we don't, it'll be too late
Time would have passed us by

Party

I made all my plans ahead
Wrote out a full guest list
I double checked it loads of times
To make sure no-one's missed

I bought balloons and streamers
To make the party fun
But didn't leave enough time
To get all my work done

With fingers, cakes and biscuits
So much I had to get
Can't forget the ice cream
Just hope the jelly's set

But I have worked so hard
I really need to stop
I've baked a lovely birthday cake
Put candles on the top

The day before the party
The house looks just like new
I've cleaned, shined and scrubbed
The floor is polished too

Today's the day of the party
And I've done all that I should
Everything is ready
And it's all looking good

And all the guests are here
The party's in full swing
All the food's been eaten
Just birthday song to sing

Well now the party's over
All dishes in the sink
But I am so tired
I must have forty winks

I have worked so very hard
My birthday has been great
But now I am exhausted
And in a real bad state

And so I have to say
It's been too much you see
Although I do like birthdays
They are no good for me

So all of you remember
This is my fervent plea
No more birthday parties
Let's just go out for tea!

The library

The library was the place to go
Whether you were rich or poor
You could borrow books to read
And come back next day for more!

And the choice was truly amazing
There were books of every kind
And it was so hard to decide
Which books to leave behind

They were all in alphabet order
Stacked from ceiling to floor
Even though some were borrowed
There would always be plenty more

And our library books were stamped
They had to be back by that date
And so we were always careful
Not to bring them back too late

And there were so many books
Some with large print, some small
And some were stacked very high
So to reach them you had to be tall

And we couldn't raise our voices
Because noise just wasn't allowed
You had to be very quiet
And make sure there wasn't a sound

Every Day May Not Be Good...

There were thousands of books to look at
None of them need be bought
You could read some when you were there
As long as the story was short

The shelves were full to the top
With books we could all take away
And if we read them too quickly
We'd get more the very next day

But these days, libraries are empty
And some have even closed down
Because people have purchased a 'kindle'
And they carry their libraries around!

Why

I had an early meeting
Planned many weeks ago
And if I was late or missed it
I'd be out of a job, you know

Each day I am up early
Before the dawn comes round
But morning of the meeting
My alarm clock made no sound!

I was waiting for a parcel
To be brought straight to my door
I stayed in all day specially
It would come I knew for sure

But though I watched the clock
Counting every chime
The parcel never did arrive
It was a waste of time!

I was going to the theatre
To see my favourite star
I walked instead of driving
As the theatre wasn't far

But as I walked down the street
I tripped and hurt my toe
And by the time I got there
I found I'd missed the show

My friend asked me for dinner
She is a brilliant cook
She made a really great meal
Without a cookery book

So I returned her invitation
And planned good things to eat
But on the night of the dinner
I overcooked the meat!

So why do these things happen
What is this all about
Why, when you try so hard
Do things still not work out

But there is no explanation
No point in saying 'why us?'
Like lots of things in life
These things are sent to try us!

Pets

Cats are very playful
They're good to have around
You never know where they are
As they don't make a sound

Gerbils are friendly pets
And they very rarely bite
They're quiet during daytime
But active over night

Dogs can be quite noisy
And annoy us when they bark
So give your dogs a treat
And take them to the park

Hamsters keep us amused
Round on the wheel they go
Faster and faster, round and round
Such clever tricks they show

A goldfish is the kind of pet
That doesn't do too much
Happily swimming in his bowl
You look, but cannot touch

A guinea pig is sociable
It likes grass and hay
It also is quite sensitive
And often hides away

Every Day May Not Be Good...

A parrot likes to imitate
When friends come to see it
You must be careful what you say
'Cos parrot might repeat it!

A rabbit is a lovely pet
It is so soft and sweet
Its favourite food is carrots
As they are good to eat

But if you want a tidy house
No mess on floor or wall
My advice to you would surely be
Don't have pets at all!

Toys

All babies love to play with toys
They never have enough
From cuddly bears and racing cars
And dogs that can go 'woof'

And bouncing balls and picture books
And music toys galore
And little trains and bath time boats
And aeroplanes that soar

We buy them lots of lovely toys
Like cars and building blocks
And open these to show to them
But they just want the box!

They surround themselves with their toys
And then when they get bored
They reach for a different one
That they earlier had ignored.

The more they have, the more we buy
Our cupboards overflow
Our home will never look the same
With all the toys on show

We try to store them tidily
To play with one by one
But baby wants them all at once
'Cos he thinks it's more fun

But when it comes to evening
We tidy up the heap
And put them all away again
Whilst baby's fast asleep

But morning comes around again
And every toy is back
Including coloured beakers
Which baby likes to stack

And though our home's untidy
And it will stay this way
We wouldn't change it for the world
'Cos baby rules, OK!

Talking

When baby first starts to talk
It's music to our ears
He makes a lot of different sounds
And copies all he hears

We listen to his lovely voice
Which makes us feel so happy
Constantly chattering to himself
Whilst we change his nappy

Talking can be good for us
In friends we can confide
And if we don't know what to do
They help us to decide

Some talk of the future
Others recall the past
Some talk really slowly
Whilst others talk too fast

And some people talk too loud
And cause us agitation
It's hard to say 'hush, please'
If they're a close relation

Some speak too soft to hear
And we keep saying 'pardon?'
It's not as if they're far away
Or we are in the garden

Every Day May Not Be Good...

A gentle voice on the 'phone
Can sooth us with its tone
Especially when they're far away
And we are on our own

And some people have the gift
To talk just with their eyes
We know exactly what they mean
With just an eyebrow rise

But just like overeating
When you need to diet
Some people always talk too much
When we need peace and quiet

Daydreams

When all the chores have been done
I take a well earned break
I let my mind go wandering
Asleep but half awake

I think of things I'd like to do
I'm really feeling great
The world is now my oyster
Whilst I'm in this dreamy state

Places I would love to see
If I could afford the trip
I'd happily fly anywhere
Or go by train or ship

My home would be so modern
Light furnishings and fixtures
I'd adorn every single wall
With great paintings and nice pictures

I'd go to all the top shows
And book a front row seat
Then I'd meet all the cast
It would be such a treat

My house would be so big
Gold handles on the door
I'd get the best designers
And have gadgets by the score

Every Day May Not Be Good...

I'd have my clothes all made
And follow current trend
I'd replace any that got torn
And never need to mend

In my chauffeur driven limo
I'd be taken to smart shops
And home with lots of purchases
Of dresses, skirts and tops

I'd go to fancy restaurants
With good food and fine wine
Anything I want to eat
It would be so divine

But suddenly I am awake
Back home from distant shores
The ball is all but over
Cinders back to do her chores!

My Extension

I needed an extension
Because my house was small
I wanted an extra room
And, a wider hall

The builders started early
Which was so good to see
But they left after lunch
To have an early tea!

They didn't come the next day
I was filled with despair
Nor the next day either
I was tearing out my hair

The weeks went by so slowly
The builders never showed
And when I tried to ring them
I got the engaged tone

After many weeks, they came
And continued my extension
But why it had been so long
They didn't even mention

The work dragged on for months
Much longer than it should
The house was a mess
Just as friends had said it would

21

When would the work be done
Would it ever be completed
I sat there in the cold and damp
'Cos the house could not be heated

At long last, came the day
When all the work was done
My house was my own again
But it had not been much fun

The work had been expensive
And the house, a building site
With bricks, stones and mortar
Around, all day and night

But all my friends are worried
They ask what's going on
They think I've lost my memory
As I've planned another one!

Chocolate

What is it about chocolate
That makes us crave for more
Is it texture or the taste
We feel we can't ignore

We try not to be greedy
One square instead of two
But that just leaves us feeling
As if we've had too few

Out of sight is out of mind
So we put it in the drawer
But this doesn't work for us
Just makes us want it more

There is a choice of chocolate
Milk or plain or white
But whichever one you choose
All three are a delight

We must forget about chocolate
But the more we try to deny
Just makes us crave it more
However hard we try

We really love our chocolate
With its delicious taste
Whenever we are given some
There's none that goes to waste!

We see chocolates of every kind
As we pass the sweet shop
And so hard to ignore them
Impossible not to stop

Yes, chocolate is just like a drug
One bite and we are lost
We have to have it badly
Regardless of the cost

So guys if you want to impress
You don't need to be a good dancer
Forget the diamonds and the pearls
'Cos chocolates are the answer!

Food

I wake up every morning
A family to feed
It's not that we eat a lot,
You couldn't call it greed

And every day I make a meal
As I do like to cook
Most days I know what to make
But sometimes I am stuck

To always ring the changes
Is quite a mammoth task
Something different every day
Is not too much to ask

I try so hard and do my best
To find some inspiration
I have the will, I have the means,
I have the motivation

And so I try my hardest
To think of something new
Something unexpected
And would be great to do

And even though my meals
Are quite predictable
The family leave the table
With tummies that are full

25

Every Day May Not Be Good...

Salmon, pizza, sausage rolls,
We've had them all before
Steak and chicken, cod and chips
We like them, that's for sure

These are meals that over time
Have been well tried and tested
These are meals that over time
Have been the most requested

But something different would be nice
I'm sure you will agree
There's only one solution here,
Let's all go out for tea!

Shopping

My favourite way of shopping
Is on the internet
Simple and straightforward
How easy can it get?

So if I want to buy something
The shops are in my sight
Their doors are always open
Morning, noon and night

I just sit at my computer,
At any time of day
Anything I want to buy
Is just a click away

There is so much to choose from
It is a great big store
Anything I want to buy
Is brought straight to my door

My heart is really pounding
What lovely things I see
I want to purchase everything
And have a spending spree

I really must have it now
Although I could have waited
It's something that I have to have
Moderation's overrated

Every Day May Not Be Good...

I can't resist the things I see
However hard I try
I see something, I want it now
And so I click to buy

The more I see, the more I want
I am quite fixated
My shopping bag is now quite full
I feel oh so elated

But what is this, oh no, please no,
My hopes once more are dashed
I get my coat to face the crowds,
The internet has crashed!

My mobile phone

My mobile phone is my new best friend,
I take it wherever I go
Someone might need me, I might get a text
Or a phone call from someone I know

I might want to chat whilst I'm on the train
Or text a very close friend
There might be some incoming post for me
Or an e-mail I want to send

I might want to check an appointment
Or arrange a time that we meet
Or I may want to book a restaurant table
Not far away, where we can eat

Or if I go to meet a good friend
Who's arriving on a late flight
I can check with the airport if she'll be on time
Or if she's due much later that night

Or I might need to check on times of trains
And I may want to book a hotel
My phone is useful in so many ways
And fits in my bag so well

Or if I'm out and someone takes ill
I can get help straight away
Because my mobile phone's with me
There will not be a moment's delay

Every Day May Not Be Good...

Or if I have arranged a meeting
And I am running a bit late
I can quickly alter the time to meet
Or change it to a new date

Wherever I am, whatever the time
Out comes my mobile phone
I look at it lovingly in my hand
And click to await the ringtone

Time stands still as I gaze at my phone
As I patiently wait to chat
But what is this, it can't be so
Oh no, the battery's flat!!

TV

There are lots of programmes
From news to films and plays
Just turn on the TV set
And while away the days

It is so very easy
And very tempting too
Especially when you're feeling down
Because you've got the flu

There's so much to choose from
There's always something on
From pottery to cookery
The list goes on and on

There's Masterchef and Mastermind
And also lots of chat
There's even one on how to sell
Your own home or your flat

Appealing to all age groups
With programmes old or new
There's even one for babies
When they're just one or two!

There are so many programmes
That we can pick and choose
From comedy to drama
Or just the evening news

Every Day May Not Be Good...

Soaps are very popular
To them we get addicted
Who will rent a new flat
And who will be evicted?

But if you have a partner
Who only wants the sport
It wouldn't be the first time
Remote control is fought

And so we have the problem
That too much choice can bring
'Cos if you do not live alone
You can't watch everything

And so my advice would be
To every bride and groom
The best solution has to be
TVs in every room!!

Memory

My memory used to be so good
My powers of recall
Shopping lists and phone numbers
I could remember all

There's nothing that I would forget
Even songs and rhymes
I never would reproach myself
I'd remember all the lines

All important dates and times
I'd remember in my head
I knew the words on every line
Of every book I'd read

But these days I have to say
My memory's gone downhill
Forgetting lots of things is bad
And making me quite ill

I go upstairs to get something
That I forgot before
But once upstairs, I forget
What I went up for

Thinking what I might have missed
Fills me with regret
What is it that I forgot
I need to go and get

Every Day May Not Be Good...

Good memory is important
I'm sure you will agree
But trying to recall the past
Is quite beyond me

So is there any answer
Can you tell me what to do
I should remember lots of things
Instead of just a few

But although I really need some help
To find out what I've missed
The answer is quite clear to see
Just make a little list!!

Holidays

We love to go on holiday
To travel far away
To see far distant lands
And enjoy a 2-week stay

We pack our bags carefully
With clothes newly bought
And set off very early
To reach the airport

We have to wait some hours
As our plane has been delayed
Oh, why did we forget
The sandwiches we made

Eventually we get on board
The aeroplane now ready
We walk quickly up the steps
It takes off slow and steady

We reach our destination
And off the plane we go
We get our passports ready
But the queue moves very slow

We arrive at our hotel
Walk in with our suitcase
Is this really what we paid for?
It is a dreadful place

The room has not been cleaned
And cobwebs everywhere
This is truly awful
And just too much to bear

The bed is very lumpy
So we sleep upon the floor
We have no running water
No lock upon the door

We really cannot live with
This poor accommodation
If we hadn't flown over here
We'd head back to the station

Our holiday was awful
The 2 weeks slowly passed
So we were all so happy
To see our home at last

So all please do remember
That wherever you may roam
Holidays can be good or bad
But there's no place like home!

Good Old Days

When I was just a teenager
I'd wear the latest fashion
I'd follow all the current trends
With unbridled passion

I'd hang out with all my friends
And go to all the clubs
We'd walk for miles in the rain
To get to bars and pubs

And Cliff and Elvis were the best
Much loved by everyone
And when they brought out records
They went straight to number one

We'd queue all night for tickets
And get soaked in a thunderstorm
But we all thought it was worth it
To see them both perform

And we couldn't afford a car
So we would have to catch the bus
And if we had a long wait
We would never made a fuss

And pennies were then worth something
And sixpence even more
And we all saved up to buy records
No matter how rich or poor

The family would get together
When it was time for tea
We'd have our meals together
But not in front of the TV!

And we were all safe when outdoors
We could play in the street or the park
There really was nothing to fear
Even late at night, after dark

But life will always be changing
With good things and bad things it's true
Best make the most of the present
Before those become good old days too!

Hotels

When we go on holiday
We need somewhere to stay
A nice hotel is lovely
When we are far away

The choice we have is great
So we are never stuck
It is really easy
To choose one and then book

Some are quite old fashioned
Whilst others are brand new
Some are very basic
But clean and bright too

Some have a swimming pool
A sauna and a gym
Some are very lavish
Whilst others are quite grim

Some have a restaurant
And a choice of food
Others have a tranquil bar
To get you in the mood

If there's many floors
I hope you have the time
'Cos if the lifts break down
You'll have a long hard climb

Every Day May Not Be Good...

You go up to your room
Tired, there's no denying
You hope that you can sleep
With no babies crying

Most hotels are good
And make your holiday
But some are very poor
And spoil your trip away

Well I love my hotel stays
I've lots more booked ahead
But it's always oh so nice
To come home to my own bed!

Can't do without!

When we go on holiday
Abroad to foreign lands
There's something that my hubby needs
You have to understand

It's something that he has to have
Whenever we're away
He simply cannot live without
And needs it every day

It has become essential
Just like food and drink
And if he couldn't get it
He wouldn't sleep a wink

He just keeps on looking
And never does complain
Even though he was caught
In the pouring rain

And when we are on holiday
Far away from home
He searches everywhere he can
And often on his own

He has to have it every day
Or else he gets so sad
To him it is important
And not a passing fad

His holiday is not complete
If he doesn't find one
It's nothing that he wants to eat
Nor something that he rides on

Have you guessed what it can be
That he can't live without
He knows he has to have it
Of that I have no doubt

And so he searches high and low
From early till much later
In case you haven't guessed by now
It's the daily newspaper!

Satisfaction

We are never satisfied
We look for pastures new
It could be something we forgot
That now we need to do

It could be a diploma
That we've worked so hard for
But when we've achieved it
We want another, even more

It could be a brand new jumper
That's made of pure new wool
But after we've worn it once
It just looks old and dull

It could even be a trip abroad
A wonderful vacation
But when we're there, all we want
Is a different destination

It may even be a top job
That we had longed for
But as soon as it is offered
We don't want it anymore

In our minds we always think
Of things we'd like to have
But when we get our heart's desire
It's just a passing fad

43

Every Day May Not Be Good...

Striving daily in the hope
That we will feel contented
Even if the car's been hired
And our house is rented

When will we reach a point
When everything's just right
I doubt that this state of mind
Will happen overnight

But if you get a bargain
Something cheap you really need
Eat your heart out Mick Jagger!
'Cos satisfaction's guaranteed!

A fly

I am a little fly
Darting here and there
I like to fly about
In the open air

I always head for flowers
And land on a petal
Any flower that is in bloom
On it, I'll gladly settle

I love the summer months
When the weather's really nice
The winter is not good for me
With all that snow and ice

A window that is open wide
I always fly through
But trying to get out again
Is very hard to do

And if a lamp is lit
When it is late at night
It's hard to stop myself
From flying to the light

I sometimes go indoors
And land softly on a wall
I hear and see what's going on
Whilst up the wall I crawl

45

And when I see a jar of jam
For me a tasty treat
It can be rather tricky
To climb out with sticky feet

A spider's web spells danger
And if there's one in sight
I'm careful where I'm flying
Or I'll be a tasty bite!

But sometimes I find myself
In a tricky spot
'Cos if I don't exit fast
I know I will be swat!

Regrets

The world would be a better place
If we had no regrets
If we could hold our heads up high
And leave no bills or debts

Regretting something that we did
Causes us great sorrow
So we must forget about it now
And think about tomorrow

Regretting something that we said
Makes us feel so bad
It hurts us really deeply
And makes us feel so sad

Regrets from years gone by
We didn't think would last
But they come back to haunt us
From some time in the past

Regretting speaking out of turn
Is something we all do
If only we could take it back
Or say it wasn't true

We may regret a harsh word
That shouldn't have been said
If only we had stayed quiet
And said nothing at all instead.

Regretting something hurts us most
And eats us up inside
And takes away our confidence
Our self worth and our pride

So we should all make very sure
Decisions are all right
So we do not regret things
That keep us up at night

And we should think before we speak
Then it won't come out all wrong
And if we do, we then can say
'Ne rien' just like the song!

Trains

Trains are quite essential
They take us near and far
What would we do without them
They're much faster than a car

And time goes by so quickly
As they rush through every station
And in the twinkling of an eye
They reach each destination

Most trains are now electric
Whilst some of them are steam
With lots and lots of carriages
Much bigger than they seem

Some have quiet coaches
Where there isn't any noise
So don't sit there with children
If they have noisy toys

There is a buffet car
If you want a bite to eat
You can go at any time
Then bring it to your seat

And if you spend more money
To be separate from the mass
You'll get free refreshments
Brought to you, in first class

Every Day May Not Be Good...

And if someone's in your seat
When you are running late
You can ask them most politely
If they would please vacate

But sometimes when it's busy
And there isn't a spare seat
You stand up all the journey
Which is hard upon your feet

And at mercy of the weather
If there is ice and snow
The train may then run late
Or, not at all, you know

But all in all, a train
Is great for all of us
It gets us where we need to go
With very little fuss

So if you want to get away
And visit a relation
Just put on your coat and hat
And head off for the station!

I woke up one morning

I woke up one morning
The sun was in the sky
It was such a warm feeling
It made my spirits high

I woke up one morning
The rain was coming down
It looked so depressing
I didn't go to town

I woke up one morning
It was a foggy day
I set off for the shops
But couldn't find the way

I woke up one morning
Too cold to leave my bed
I had things to do
But stayed there instead

I woke up one morning
The wind was really blowing
I battled to the shops
My cheeks were really glowing

I woke up one morning
To a layer of snow
I needed to go out
But was too cold to go

Every Day May Not Be Good...

I woke up one morning
There was thunder overhead
And as the lightning flashed
I was glad I was in bed

I woke up one morning
The sky was very grey
I went out in the rain
But came back straight away

So the moral of the story
Is oh so plain to see
We cannot change the weather
'Cos what will be, will be

Shopping

A trip to the supermarket
'Cos my stocks are low
I write down what I want
And then off I go

I have quite a choice
And I can pick and choose
So which one shall I go to
As they all have such long queues

And they all sell the same things
With their own brands too
I really like them all
So any of them will do

Shall I choose a large store
Though longer to get round
Or perhaps a small one,
Goods easy to be found

Shall I go to Tesco
But Sainsbury's is nearer
Or shall it be Asda
'Cos Morrisons' is dearer

They all have their merits
All are very good
I wish I could just choose one
But don't know which I should

Every Day May Not Be Good...

And indecision is so bad
I've found out to my cost
You know the well known saying
He who hesitates is lost

My shopping list is long
And I don't have much time
So which store shall I go to
For all my food and wine

And so I have the answer
My dilemma now will stop
I'll just pop down the road
To my local shop!

Board games

There are lots of board games
That we all like to play
They keep us fully occupied
And pass the time away

Everyone likes board games
Whatever age you may be
And some games go on so long
They finish well after tea!

And playing lots of board games
Gives us lots of fun
They'll be forever popular
For many years to come

Scrabble is a board game
That really tests your mind
It makes you think of words
That are very hard to find

There is a great board game
It's called Monopoly
And you are given money
To purchase property

Another game is Ludo
It is so very nice
Though it's very basic
With counters and a dice

Every Day May Not Be Good...

Some like snakes and ladders
Up and down you go
And the journey to the top
Can be very slow

Chess is stimulating
You plan your moves and wait
And when they least expect it
You shout out 'checkmate!'

Another game is 'Draughts'
It sometimes makes you frown
But then you start to smile again
Because you've got a crown!

Yes, Board games sure are great
When you have got a hoard
But playing them too often
Is bound to make you 'bored!"

Crosswords

We love to fill in crosswords
Working out the clues
Some are easy some are hard
Which one would you choose?

We find them in the newspaper
Some large and some are small
But those that are in the Times
Are hardest of them all!

Some would take us ages
But we never would give up
Determined to complete them
Drinking tea, cup after cup

So engrossed, we'd miss a meal
Until it was complete
And only then would we stop
And have a bite to eat

We used to work out answers
And fill them in, in pen
But if most of them were wrong
We'd have to start again

Our partners would do them too
But then if they got stuck
They'd ask us to come and help
And we would take a look

Every Day May Not Be Good...

We'd wrack our brains and try to think
Of something that would fit
But before long we'd realise
That that just wasn't it

We'd sit down together
But argue over clues
We each thought that we were right
We had our own views

And when we did them jointly
Raised voices could be heard
But now we do them separately
There's never a cross word!

Jumping to conclusions

We all jump to conclusions
Instead of giving thought
We judge people wrongly
Then apology is sought

We all jump to conclusions
Because we are seeing red
And they say 'Fools rush in,
Where angels fear to tread'

We all jump to conclusions
And think we're always right
And realising we got it wrong
Keeps us up at night

We all jump to conclusions
Instead of thinking twice
We put our foot in it
And say something that's not nice

We're very quick to judge
And then we get quite mad
When our friend is late
Because the traffic's bad

We're angry if he doesn't come
At the time he said
It never does occur to us
He might be ill in bed

Every Day May Not Be Good...

We shout if our seat's taken
We really shouldn't do it
'Cos it is our own fault
That others beat us to it

We are annoyed if our train
Doesn't run on time
But what we didn't know
Was that snow was on the line

So we should be more careful
And make sure we're not heard
Wait until the facts are known
Before we say a word

Why

Why is it when we buy a dress
Tried on, it was just right
But when we get it home that day
We find that it's too tight

Why is it when we make a list
Of things we need a lot
But when we finish and get home
Always something we've forgot

Why is it when we change a bulb
As one of them has gone
Within a day or two of that
There goes another one

Why is it when we make a plan
To picnic out of doors
Every day the sun shines bright
But on that day, it pours

Why is it when we're not dressed
As we are on our own
An unexpected guest arrives
Who didn't check by phone

Why is it when we need to park
And really have to dash
The exact payment is needed
But we haven't got the cash

Every Day May Not Be Good...

Why is it when we're partying
And neighbours hate the din
We invite them to join us
But they will not come in

I ask myself why oh why
My plans are all thwarted
But sadly these things happen
So I have to get it sorted

So just get on with life
No point in asking 'why us?'
'Cos there really is no doubt
These things are sent to try us!

Dancing

Dancing is enjoyable
And very good for you
And there are lots of dances
That all of us can do

Foxtrot, waltz and quickstep
The dances we all know
But you have to be so careful
Not to tread on partner's toe!

And if you want to barn dance
My favourite one, by far
Just take your partner by the hand
And tip your hat, yee har!!

Line dancing is really great
Another love of mine
Just put on your cowboy boots
And all get in a line!

Zumba dance is popular
It really keeps you fit
It can leave you out of breath
Whilst keeping up with it!

Another dance that's naughty
And not so much discussed
Is Pole dancing and talked about
With voices that are hushed

Every Day May Not Be Good...

And if you want to break dance
Down on the floor you go
It's very energetic
And makes a good floor show!

And then there's ballet dancing
Which can make your feet ache
So if it does, just take a break
And go and watch Swan Lake!

So, music, maestro, if you please,
And trip the light fandango
A willing partner's all you need
'Cos it takes two to tango!

Other peoples lives

We are all very interested
In lots of different things
From newspaper items
To who is having flings!

What is the latest film?
And when does it come out?
Who is starring in it?
And what is it about?

Which book's just been published?
And can I get a copy?
Is it a good thriller?
Or a romance that is soppy?

What is the latest gossip?
Which film star over-dosed?
Who won today's elections
And received the most votes?

Who went to a casino
And lost all his money
And which comedian had a fall
Which wasn't very funny

Who's got into trouble?
And is an alcoholic?
Who has had a baby?
And which baby has got colic?

And who has got an Oscar?
The one we most admire
And who was charged with arson?
As they started a fire

So are we too concerned
With what other people do
Does it really matter
What they're getting up to

So if you hear some gossip
Please don't get on the phone
Leave others to their own lives
And you just live your own!

Always late

Why is it some people
Are always late, you know
They try to be on time
But they are always slow

They have an appointment
They know they must keep
They set their alarm clock
But then they oversleep

So they order a taxi
A deadline to make
But they're not ready
And the taxi has to wait

When they need to be
Early for a test
They arrive far too late
Long after all the rest

It is most annoying
When we make a plan
That if I can be on time
I'm sure that they can

They note in their diaries
A most important date
But forget all about it
And get there far too late

And if they had a meeting
That they needed to attend
They would miss the bus
And arrive at the end

They will never change
They cannot hurry up
They finish their tea
Then have another cup!

They apologise profusely
And feel so very bad
But they cannot help it
It is so very sad

So I will advise you
That in the long term
It is the early bird
That catches the worm!

Food partners

There are many foods
That are partners in life
They just go together
Like husband and wife

Some say toast and jam
Is what they have each day
And you won't be hungry
If you start the day this way

Spaghetti and meat balls
Are so enjoyable
And we leave the table
Feeling really full

And Wimbledon, we know
Would just not be the same
Without strawberry's and cream
We'd not enjoy the game

And children's favourites
Custard and jelly
They enjoy it even more
In front of the telly!

And what would life be like
If we couldn't have our fix
Of our take away favourites
Those lovely fish and chips!

And if I cook some lamb
I'd be faced with divorce
If I dared to forget
That tasty mint sauce

And if it is a cold day
Just have something nice
Something that is really hot
Like curry and rice

So all of us should strive
To be like partner food
And always 'get together'
When we are in the mood!

The taxi driver

When I was courting
Before I was a bride
I asked my boyfriend
If he could well provide

He said that he drove taxis
And he was qualified
And being very honest
On that, I had relied

One day when we were driving
I knew that he had lied
Because he hit somebody
Who very nearly died

And when we got home
He broke down and cried
He was so remorseful
That cannot be denied

I gave him another chance
And said I'm on his side
And he promised to be honest
And my worries put aside

But he wasn't truthful
Although he really tried
Some people can be like that
And won't admit they lied

So should I stay with him
I had to decide
He had tested my patience
And had hurt my pride

I just had to leave him
And had to step aside
I had done my very best
I really had tried

So if you need to take a cab
Make sure he's qualified
Because you might regret it
And be taken for a ride!

Trials and tribulations

It should have been a quiet day
A day for contemplation
A time for restfulness and peace
A time for relaxation

But sadly it was not to be
In fact, was quite the reverse
Instead of being a good day
It was really one of the worse

It began with a ring at the doorbell
So I answered but no one was there
It got me up at the crack of dawn
Probably a childhood dare

Being woken up so abruptly
Had put me in quite a bad mood
And so I went down to the kitchen
To make myself lots of nice food

I began to eat some cornflakes
But oh dear, they made me cough
The taste was just so awful
'Cos the milk had badly gone off

I went upstairs for a shower
I'd feel much better after that
But as I was going to the bathroom
I stumbled and tripped on the mat

Every Day May Not Be Good...

I needed to go to the shops
So I got the bus into town
But just as I got to the store
They were pulling the shutters down

I tried to flag down a taxi
An empty one slowed as I looked
But then he wound down his window
And said that the taxi was booked

I got home when it was dark
Then put my key into the lock
I reached out to turn on the light
But stumbled, and fainted with shock

By now I was ready for bed
This bad day had come to an end
I had no doubt that tomorrow
I surely would be on the mend

But just as I fell fast asleep
Glad that this bad day was done
Someone was ringing the doorbell
The day ended just as it begun

Wishes

If only I had a new house
And a garden with plenty of flowers
I'd sit outside on warm summer nights
And minutes would turn into hours

If only I had a big black cat
That followed wherever I went
I'd give her all my attention
And I know she'd be quite content

If only I had my own villa
In a hot country such as Spain
My friends could come and stay with me
Away from the cold wind and rain

If only I had a racing car
That moved with the speed of light
People would watch as I drove by
It would be a wonderful sight

If only I had a diamond ring
That sparkled in the sunshine
I'd polish it gleaming every day
Keep it free from the dirt and the grime

If only I could go abroad
Far away to a foreign land
I would swim in the sea all day long
Go barefoot on the golden sand

If only I had a masters degree
What a wonderful job I would get
I would soon earn enough money
To never have any debt

If only I had my own yacht
I'd sail from coast to coast
All my friends would join me
And I'd be the perfect host

So we should all stop wishing
And getting ourselves in a state
'Cos we know that all good things
Come to those who wait!!

A little friend

I have a tiny little friend
I take wherever I go
It's with me every day and night
But not something that I show

You're free to guess at what it is
I'll tell you if you get it
I guarantee that you'll be wrong
It'll bother you if you let it

It's something that I won't give up
It's been with me so long
I need it with me all the time
It keeps me calm and strong

I've had it many, many years
It's been a friend for me
I can't be parted from it
It's part of me, you see

It's something that I have to have
I love it quite completely
I gaze at it all the time
And smile at it so sweetly

When I wake up in the morning
I check that it's still there
As one day I misplaced it
But found it on the chair

Every Day May Not Be Good...

If you were me, you'd surely see
It's something really grand
It's something that is quite small
And fits nicely in my hand

I have to keep it with me
Until my dying day
Then those that I leave behind
Will understand my way

My legacy will linger on
And someone else will take it
They'll want it to bring them luck
Although they cannot make it

Have you guessed what it is?
It's my lucky charm, you see
And no one else can use it
'Cos it only works for me!

I wouldn't change a thing

I don't like the heavy rain
It dampens everything
But it helps the flowers grow
I wouldn't change a thing

I don't like the constant buzz
Of queen bees, when they sting
Their honey is so sweet and pure
I wouldn't change a thing

I don't like the winter time
I always wish for spring
Kids enjoy their snowball fights
I wouldn't change a thing

I don't like the awful din
Of alarm clocks when they ring
As they wake us up in time
I wouldn't change a thing

I don't like the smell of paint
When there's decorating
But when it's dry, it looks so good
I wouldn't change a thing

I don't like the sound of horns
I find them so annoying
But as they warn us that they're there
I wouldn't change a thing

Every Day May Not Be Good...

I don't like the deafening sound
When ambulance sirens ring
But as they save so many lives
I wouldn't change a thing

I don't like dentists drills
The fearful thoughts they bring
But as they help us keep our teeth
I wouldn't change a thing

I would not like my partner
If he ever had a fling
Some things are unforgivable
And does change everything!!

Other peoples lives

We are all very interested
In lots of different things
From newspaper items
To who is having flings!

What is the latest film?
And when does it come out?
Who is starring in it?
And what is it about?

Which book's just been published?
And can I get a copy?
Is it a good thriller?
Or a romance that is soppy?

What is the latest gossip?
Which film star over-dosed?
Who won today's elections
And received the most votes?

Who went to a casino
And lost all his money
And which comedian had a fall
Which wasn't very funny

Who's got into trouble?
And is an alcoholic?
Who has had a baby?
And which baby has got colic?

Every Day May Not Be Good...

And who has got an Oscar?
The one we most admire
And who was charged with arson?
As they started a fire

So are we too concerned
With what other people do
Does it really matter
What they're getting up to

So if you hear some gossip
Please don't get on the phone
Leave others to their own lives
And you just live your own!

Sleep

We all have those nights
When sleep just won't come
When we're really tired
And the day is nearly done

We toss and turn for hours
As we lie there in our bed
With thoughts of the day
Running through our head

We really do need sleep
But lay there in the dark
And we do not want to be
Up early with the lark!

So we start counting minutes
As they slowly tick by
Which soon turn into hours
The longer that we lie

The night goes on so long
We've tried counting sheep
And soon begin to wonder
If we'll ever fall asleep

And yet still time goes by
And we've not even dozed
We lie there in our bed
With our eyes tightly closed

Every Day May Not Be Good...

We know that we are tired
'Cos we yawn and yawn
But sleep just won't come
And now it's nearly dawn

So there's really nothing for it
We have to give up trying
And we make our way downstairs
As we're so tired of lying

Then we turn on the TV
And curl up in a heap
And in just a couple of minutes
We are sound asleep!

Indulge

We sit down at the table
And see a lovely spread
It's not that we are greedy
Or that we're not well fed

So why do we hold back
And you know we always do
So although we want more
We have one instead of two

It's so hard to resist
Chocolates and ice creams
We can have it all
But only in our dreams

It is really tempting
And looks so very good
So why do we hold back
Because we think we should

But why should we stop ourselves
Enjoying all our food
Especially as it puts us in
A really happy mood

The food looks so delicious
Why should we resist
If we do not eat it
We'll wonder what we missed

Every Day May Not Be Good...

We are told all the time
That these foods are so bad
And yet they're so delicious
The best we've ever had

So why should we deny ourselves
That really lovely treat
And it looks so delicious
And will be good to eat

So go ahead and have it
You know that you should
'Cos a little of what you fancy
Always does you good!

Football

What is it about football
That gets folks all worked up
They can talk for hours
About who'll win the FA Cup

Discussions start off quietly
But then become quite heated
'It should have been a penalty"
'You know that we were cheated!'

And then when someone scores
The fans stand up and cheer
But supporters of the rival team
Only boo and jeer!

It is an institution
That is many years old
Lots of matches played
And many tickets sold

Fans will travel anywhere
Just to see their team play
And will go to every match
Whether it's home or away

Football takes priority
And it has to come first
Even if their chosen team
Is really one of the worst

Every Day May Not Be Good...

What would we do without it
The highs and lows it brings
It's one of life's great pleasures
Amongst some other things!

You just can't beat the thrill
Of going to see a game
'Cos watching it on TV
Can never be the same!

So all you wives and girlfriends
Don't put him to the test
'Cos when it comes to choosing
He'll say that football's best!

'Cos if we left our partners
They'd cope, no doubt about it
But when it comes to football
They couldn't live without it

New Parents

Worrying as it nears the big day
Will baby be perfect in every way
Worrying when they cry in their cot
Are they too cold or are they too hot
Worrying when they start solid food
Is it enough, and should it be chewed
Worrying when they begin to crawl
Just in case they bump into the wall
Worrying when they walk by themselves
They might trip into the kitchen shelves
Worrying when they're at school without us
Hoping they're happy and won't make a fuss
Worrying when they sit their exams
Hope they remember their units and grams
Worrying when they're on their first date
Hoping they don't come home too late
Worrying when they become man and wife
Will they be happy for the rest of their life
Worrying when their baby is due
Full circle…. A new little life starts a-new

Grandparents

Not worrying when our grandchild is born
It heralds the start of a brand new dawn
Not worrying if baby cries, all babies do
It's to have our attention and that's normal, too.
Not worrying when they begin solid food
'Cos they'll eat anything baked, fried or stewed
Not worrying when they first start to crawl
They'll learn to avoid large things in the hall
Not worrying when they walk by themselves
I sure they won't bump into low level shelves
Not worrying when the school is in sight
They'll enjoy learning to read and to write
Not worrying when the exam time is near
We know they will pass and have nothing to fear
Not worrying when they're on their first date
It may even turn out to be their soul mate
Not worrying when they go tie the knot
We know they'll be happy with all that they've got
Not worrying when their baby is due
'Cos full circle, they'll learn not to worry, too!

Telepathy

Astrology and Tarot cards
And also horoscopes
Some people believe in them
It gives them such high hopes

Some think that our future
Is written in the stars
Do women come from Venus?
And do men come from Mars?

Some go to a fortune teller
And believe all that is said
Whilst others go to Palmists
To have their palms read

They want to learn their destiny
From tea leaves in a cup
But others are quite sceptical
And think it's all made up

One thing is indisputable
It's called telepathy
Our thoughts to communicate
If you try it, you will see

When someone's in your thoughts
You've not seen for a year
The phone rings and you answer
And it's their voice that you hear!

Every Day May Not Be Good...

When you're sitting in the theatre
And an old friend comes to mind
You just can't believe it
He's in the row behind!

When a friend is in trouble
You're aware of his plight
Like a sixth sense, you feel it
Something's not quite right

Some call it a coincidence
But I strongly disagree
Air waves all around us
And it's called telepathy

You can transfer your thoughts
You don't need to write or call
But make sure that they're nice ones
Or you'll have no friends at all!

Guardian angels

We all have guardian angels
They keep us safe from harm
They're always there beside us
Just like a lucky charm

Although we cannot see them
They help us on our way
They watch all the things we do
And are there for us each day

And our guardian angels
Are there whatever we do
They are like our shadows
Where we go, they'll go too

And our guardian angels
Are always by our side
And because they are invisible
They do not need to hide

They'll always be there for us
And if we go astray
They'll be our guiding light
And help us on our way

And if we need their help
They're honest and they're just
We rely on them completely
In them we put our trust

And it is so reassuring
To know that they are there
And that they will protect us
And that they'll always care

So as we go through life
Making choices every day
They are there beside us
And help us on our way

And so thank you guardian angels
We have so much love for you
And when our lives are over
We'll be guardian angels too!

Exams

We always try our best
In everything we do
At school and university
And in our work place, too

We have always been told
That we must do our best
And now has come the time
To put it to the test

We've tried our hardest
To learn all that we can
So that when the big day's here
We will pass our exam

We stay up late to study
When others are in bed
We memorise the answers
To keep them in our head

We ask our friends to test us
To see if we are right
And if it is beyond us
Keep at it through the night

We give up our social life
To concentrate on learning
Our nerves are getting to us
And our stomach's churning

Every Day May Not Be Good...

We go from book to book
Checking as we go
Making sure we don't miss out
On what we need to know

The exams are getting nearer
And we're getting stressed
Even though it's very hard
We will do our best

But if we don't pass this time
And if not now, then when
'Cos if at first you don't succeed
Just try and try again!

The Joiner

I needed a joiner
To repair a broken chest
He arrived very late
Wearing jeans and a vest

I showed him the work
He said he would do it
And he took out his tools
and then set to it

But three hours later
The joiner was still here
He was sat in the lounge
Drinking a can of beer!

I told him to hurry up
'Cos it was getting late
He said I shouldn't worry
As he was doing great

But one hour later
He said he'd finish soon
But two hours later
He was whistling a tune

Eventually he finished
And I paid him what was due
He said that the chest
Was now as good as new

So when he had gone
I went to check it out
The chest was still broken!
He knew that, I've no doubt

So I rang up the joiner
And said it wasn't funny
He should come back straight away
And give me back my money

He said it was his drill
And he didn't have the screw
He didn't have his hammer
And the nail was bent, too

But don't believe a word of it
And don't take us for fools
Because as the saying goes
A bad workman blames his tools!

Interesting people

There are lots of people
Whom we all admire
We follow all they do
And to them we do aspire

We love the Royal family
In particular, the Queen
She's an amazing lady
The best there's ever been

We're interested in politics
And listen to debates
Some like David Cameron
And think he's really great

And what about Cliff Richard
He is still going strong
He sang in the rain at Wimbledon
So we could sing along

And if you could meet a star
Which one would you choose
Would it be Nicole Kidman
Or perhaps Tom Cruise

We all like Prince William
And lovely Kate too
They make a great couple
And we follow all they do

Every Day May Not Be Good...

And it is very interesting
When Madonna's in the news
Exercising to be slim
But what's she got to loose?

It's interesting to know
What David Beckham's doing
And is Simon Cowell here
And are the people queuing

But don't envy famous people
Nor ones that have great wealth
'Cos the most interesting person
Is, of course, yourself!

Food

Food is a subject
That is talked about a lot
Some foods are good for you
Whilst other foods are not

We should all eat good food
To keep us well and fit
But do not eat a huge meal
Nor a tiny bit

We have to strive for balance
So that what we eat's just right
And stop when we are full
Without that extra bite

Some people eat too much
Which is a big mistake
It doesn't do them any good
Just gives them tummy ache

But food is good for us
And we have it every day
And when we are starving
We need it straight away

And we have to watch our diet
To eat just what we need
Because if we eat too much
Some would call it greed

And if we eat too little
And loose too much weight
This can be just as bad
As if we over ate

And so if you have got
A lot upon your plate
I hope that it's not too much
Or you'll end up in a state

And if you've had enough
This is my advice to you
You'd better not bite off
More than you can chew!

E-mails

It's great to send e-mails
It saves us so much time
My friend sends me an email
And then I send him mine

And we can send our e-mail
Any time, night or day
Happy in the knowledge
It will get there straight away

It arrives in our in-box
Ready for us to see
And we send off our reply
And everything is free

We can type out all our mail
And then we click on 'send'
And when we have finished
We log out at the end

What would we do without it
Normal mail is very slow
Letters would be delayed
Post Office queues would grow

And stamps would cost a lot
And we would all complain
And postmen would go on strike
And then not be seen again!

And letters would be lost
And parcels go astray
And no one would be happy
At the long delay

But sometimes it may happen
That a virus gets our mail
And takes over our address
Sending spam throughout its trail

So starting up a new one
Is all that we can do
Until the same thing happens
And that gets a virus too!

Supermarkets

There are lots of supermarkets
And everything they sell
We see them all over
And they all do very well

And they sell so many things
You really can't resist
And you buy so much more
Than those upon your list

And so it's very tempting
When you go into the store
Instead of buying one
You end up buying more

There are daily offers
Displayed for all to see
They're so hard to resist
Buy one, get one free

And so you buy everything
Whilst the offer is on
Because next time you come
Those items will be gone

And all the food is laid out
For maximum appeal
But are you really getting
Such a good deal?

And when you have finished
You have to join the line
Checkouts are always slow
And takes such a long time

And you just can't resist
There is so much to take
But then carrying it home
Makes your back ache!

And so my advice to you
To save money and a queue
Order everything online
And get them brought to you!

Hobbies

There are lots of hobbies
Of every different kind
They help to pass the time
And occupy our mind

And they can be profitable
If they go a long way back
Such as collecting antiques
Or stamps like penny black

Collecting is enjoyable
And interesting to do
And there are lots of things
To be collected, too

Such as dolls house miniatures
Some would call cute
And collecting is fun
And a really great pursuit

A hobby such as painting
Can give so much pleasure
And can be done at any time
Regardless of the weather

Writing poetry's really great
And occupies your mind
Some are written quickly
Whilst others take more time

Learning to play an instrument
Is really quite fulfilling
And you could perform on stage
As long as you are willing

Extra qualifications
Can never be a chore
And gaining a degree
Is what you do it for

So come on all you people
Make your spare time great
By taking up something new
Before it is too late!

A problem

I had a little problem
It wouldn't go away
It was always on my mind
Every night and day

The problem was apparent
How could I make it go
I just had to hide it
So that no one would know

It began quite suddenly
And caught me by surprise
I was quite astounded
At the problem's size

I had to deal with it
Which was hard to do
I'm sure you'd feel the same
If it happened to you

The problem just got bigger
I was worried even more
But others just kept saying
What are you worrying for

Problems present themselves
Quite out of the blue
And you really have to know
Exactly what to do

And even if our friends
Know what it's all about
Sometimes they're not able
To sort the problem out

And so we have to think
Of where to go from here
And hope that a solution
Will suddenly appear

So life is full of problems
That is very true
But trying to resolve them
Has become a problem too!

Double meanings

Tea can mean dinner time
Some call it supper
But in my mind tea just means
It's time for a cuppa!

A plaster is needed
If you have a fall
But it really is essential
For patching up a wall

A coach ride will take you
Wherever you want to go
And a coach can teach you
All you want to know

A banger is a firework
Lit on bonfire night
But it can be a sausage
That makes a tasty bite

A copper is a policeman
Doing his daily rounds
But can also be old money
240 to the pound

A roast is always known as
A joint of well cooked meat
But if you roast, it could mean
That you've had too much heat

Every Day May Not Be Good...

A sweet is very nice to suck
And good it makes you feel
But a sweet can also be
Dessert after a meal

A car's bonnet is at the front
And at the back, the boot
And when baby's bonnet's on
She looks really cute

So when we say something
And this I must repeat
Make sure we're all singing
From the same hymn sheet!

Activities

Walking is good for you
And keeps you really fit
And being in the fresh air
Is quite a benefit

Swimming is good for you
And it is so much fun
And a nice way to cool off
When you've had too much sun

Skipping is good for you
And keeps you really fit
Though it makes you breathless
And tires you quite a bit

Cycling is good for you
Especially up a hill
And to keep the bike moving
Requires a lot of skill

Tennis is good for you
And keeps you on your toes
But keep your eye on the ball
To hit wherever it goes

Rowing is good for you
Although you mostly sit
Your arms get a full workout
And keeps you really fit

Badminton is good for you
An exhilarating sport
You have to be nimble on your feet
As you run around the court

Gymnastics is good for you
But not easy to do
You have to be quite flexible
And strong and agile too

But if these things are not for you
'Cos you're feeling out of sorts
You can enjoy, without a doubt
Spectator sports, of course!

Traffic

The day had started quietly
With not a soul awake
I was going on my holiday
To have a well earned break

I set off very early
To avoid the big long queues
But what I didn't think of doing
Was checking the traffic news

'Cos as I joined the motorway
Expecting no delays
I saw that this would be
One of my very bad days

The queues were so very long
As far as the eye could see
And in a hot and stuffy car
How awful this would be

Is this really what I wanted
I'm hardly moving at all
And at this snail's pace
My car is likely to stall

This is so unpleasant
I just can't take much more
I wish I hadn't stepped out
From my own front door

Every Day May Not Be Good...

So there is nothing for it
But to turn the car around
And get away from the crowd
And then be homeward bound

It would have been so stressful
To continue on my way
With hours of sitting in the car
On this very hot day

The best holiday for me right now
Is staring me in the face
The happiest time will surely be
At home in my own place

Lucky charms

When I was out walking
I saw a four leaf clover
I knew it would bring me luck
And I felt good all over

When I was out walking
I saw a big black cat
I knew it would bring me luck
And so I gave it a quick pat

When I was out walking
I saw a bright new pin
I knew it would bring me luck
So I walked home with a grin

When I was out walking
A rabbit's foot I spied
I knew it would bring me luck
My smile I couldn't hide

When I was out walking
A stranger smiled at me
That was all I needed
And I smiled back, you see

When I was out walking
A gypsy gave me some heather
I knew it would bring me luck
My heart was light as a feather

Every Day May Not Be Good...

When I was out walking
I saw a shiny horse shoe
I knew it would bring me luck
And my happiness grew and grew

When I was out walking
I saw a beggar under a tree
So I gave him all my lucky charms
'Cos he needed them more than me

Obsession

Some say it is problem
That is shared by many folk
David Beckham has it too
And Posh just has to cope

Tidiness rules their life
Everything in its place
Everything the right way round
And all the same way face

It isn't always obvious
But it is always there
And those that are very close
Do soon become aware

All books in the bookcase
No newspapers on the floor
'Cos those that are so tidy
Do not find it a chore

This obsession rules their life
As mess they can't ignore
Everything in its place
And each item in its drawer

They can't relax at all
If something is around
That should be put away
And not lying on the ground

They find it hard to concentrate
When everything's a mess
Piled up upon the floor
A skirt, a blouse, a dress

They cannot bear untidiness
And have to pick it up
They put away the dishes
Right to the very last cup

But folks I have the answer
You can send these guys to me
They can tidy up my house
For a handsome fee or free!

A good deed

I had a big dilemma
I had promised to help out
Doing things for others
That's what life's all about

But when I gave my word
And my word is my bond
Another friend needed help
So I said I'd go along

So there was I confused
I didn't know what to do
I'd said I'd do my best
To not one friend, but two

And both on the same day
I'd promised faithfully
But couldn't be in two places
At the exact same time, you see

Didn't want to say I can't
To either friend, you know
It really was my own fault
I should not have said I'd go

So what should I do
I shouldn't have agreed
I shouldn't have said I'd go
Though both were so in need

Every Day May Not Be Good...

I couldn't choose between them
Nor pick one or the other
Both were close to me
Like sister and a brother

So there was nothing for it
Only had myself to blame
I had to let them both down
And hung my head in shame

So if you have a diary
And don't want to come unstuck
Check all of your commitments
So you don't double book!

Sleep on it

I needed to decide
Something didn't fit
Shall I take it back
No, I'll sleep on it!

I had to give a speech
Something with some wit
I needed some advice
I think I'll sleep on it!

I craved a cigarette
Even though I'd quit
So I went straight up to bed
Best to sleep on it!

My friend was expecting
Bootees I thought I'd knit
But the wool all got knotted
So, I had to sleep on it!

I had a big workout
But got tired so had to sit
I was so exhausted
So had to sleep on it!

I cut down a large tree
But got served with a writ
Nothing I could do
Except to sleep on it!

The snow was coming down
I didn't have any grit
So went straight back to bed
And had to sleep on it!

I wanted to indulge
Only just a little bit
But to curb the urge
I had to sleep on it!

I wrote my own song
And, wow, it was a hit
And now I'm in demand!
I've no time to sleep on it?

Favourite things

We all have favourite things
That we really love to do
We do them whenever we can
And it makes us feel happy too

Such as going out to the theatre
To see a really good show
It can quickly raise our mood
Whenever we're feeling low

And going out to a restaurant
To have good food and fine wine
Can always raise our spirits
And make us feel just fine

And also going on holiday
To get away from it all
It can really give us the freedom
To let our hair down and have a ball

And we can take up a good hobby
Doing something that we like
It could be something quite hard
Or easy, like flying a kite

Perhaps it is something musical
Such as learning to play a keyboard
It will give us something to do
To make sure that we don't get bored

Collecting something unusual
Something that might be quite rare
We could go out and find even more
Perhaps at a nearby swap fair

But if space is a big problem
A garage is a good place to store
Because if you don't have a car
What else would you use it for

And there are so many hobbies
Deserving of some shed room
But, folks, my favourite pastime's
Undoubtedly in the bedroom!

Good Deed

I live in a very big house
All on my very own
My house has six small bedrooms
A television and a 'phone

My aunt had been unwell
And couldn't get by on her own
So I invited her to stay
So she wouldn't be all alone

My cousin had had a fall
And was feeling very sad
So I invited him to stay
So that he wouldn't feel so bad

My brother was visiting England
He lived far away in Spain
So I invited him to stay
Though he didn't much like the rain

My sister needed company
As her husband was away
So I invited her to stay
She came the very next day

My friend was getting divorced
And she had to leave her home
So I invited her to stay
So she wouldn't be on her own

My uncle had bought a new house
But it needed work to be done
So I invited him to stay
As builders around isn't fun

And so, every one of my bedrooms
Were all now going to be used
I had invited too many people
I had really got quite confused

Though I started with good intentions
It wasn't meant to be this way
But now there's no room for me,
So a hotel is where I'll stay!

A detective story

One thing I like to do
Instead of having to cook
Is settle in my favourite chair
With an exciting 'who-dunnit' book

I go to car boot sales
And leave all my chores
To look for detective stories
From the second-hand book stores

And when I find my book
I just can't put it down
It is my favourite pastime
Much better than going to town

I get so engrossed in the pages
I just can't put it away
I often forget what the time is
And even forget what day

The story is engrossing
I have to read every word
The door bell may be ringing
I am oblivious, and haven't heard

I have to keep on going
Until the last word is read
Unaware the dinner's burning
Or that the dog should be fed

Every Day May Not Be Good...

And as time passes by
I have read every line
Not to be diverted
With neither good food nor wine

I turn page after page
Who can the villain be
Reading as fast as I can
Because I can't wait to see

And now I'm nearing the end
And I'm on the very last page
It really is so exciting
Especially at this late stage

I want to know who did it
Who struck the final blow
But oh no, the last page is missing
And now I'll never know